Big Hairy Audacious Goal

Achieving Your Deepest Desires
Before It's Too Late ...

Dr ANNE BUTCHER

First published by Ultimate World Publishing 2023
Copyright © 2023 Anne Butcher

ISBN

Paperback: 978-1-922982-36-0
Ebook: 978-1-922982-37-7

Anne Butcher has asserted her rights under the Copyright, Designs and Patents Act 1988 to be identified as the author of this work. The information in this book is based on the author's experiences and opinions. The publisher specifically disclaims responsibility for any adverse consequences which may result from use of the information contained herein. Permission to use information has been sought by the author. Any breaches will be rectified in further editions of the book.

All rights reserved. No part of this publication may be reproduced, stored in or introduced into a retrieval system, or transmitted in any form, or by any means (electronic, mechanical, photocopying, recording or otherwise) without the prior written permission of the author. Any person who does any unauthorised act in relation to this publication may be liable to criminal prosecution and civil claims for damages. Enquiries should be made through the publisher.

Cover design: Ultimate World Publishing
Layout and typesetting: Ultimate World Publishing
Editor: Vanessa McKay
Hair: Hair 'n' Beauty @ Sam's
Make-up: Funk It Up
Photography: Catherine Zamparutti SMP Photography

Acknowledgement to Jim Collins creator of #BHAG

Ultimate World Publishing
Diamond Creek,
Victoria Australia 3089
www.writeabook.com.au

Testimonials

Meeting Anne three years ago at one of my events and seeing where she is today in such a short time is nothing short of astounding. Anne set out to write her first book on her life story through the Ultimate 48 Hour Author program and achieved a massive goal not many people ever give themselves permission to do.

Next she saw the potential on how to leverage this book into a new business and went on to speak publicly and now has a fully booked one to one coaching practice with a transition towards more group work so that she can help as many people as possible achieve their big hairy audacious goals.

She is a wonderful person, that cares for people and has had herself a fair share of roadblocks she had to overcome to get to where she is today. Follow Anne's recipe if you want fast life-changing results in your life. It's never too late to go for your Big Hairy Audacious Goal.

Natasa Denman
(CEO/Founder of Ultimate 48 Hour Author)

"Anne is an insatiable learner with a servant's heart. Her wealth of knowledge, combined with her passion to help others, is her superpower."

Janelle Johnston
Master Coach, Speaker and Trainer
www.janellejohnston.com.au

"Anne has a knack of turning something big and scary into something that isn't so frightening after all.

She breaks a giant task down into small, workable sections so that it feels achievable. She combines her theoretical knowledge with real life and as such offers coaching and mentoring that can be used in the real world. She encourages, she supports, she empowers … and once she is in your corner, she's always in your corner. If you trust Anne with your biggest dreams and greatest goals … she WILL help you achieve it."

Tegan Philpott
Chief of Staff ABC Tropical North

Contents

Testimonials	iii
Dedication	1
Introduction	3
Chapter 1: How Did I End Up Here?	7
Chapter 2: Lights, Camera, Action!	17
Chapter 3: Finding Your Sensei	29
Chapter 4: Slaying The Dragon	39
Chapter 5: Diamonds In The Rough	49
Chapter 6: In The Groove	63
Chapter 7: Wave Riding And Boundaries	77
Chapter 8: Celebrating Your Wins	85
Chapter 9: Changing Lanes	93
Chapter 10: Never Give Up	101
About The Author	111
Reference List	113
Offers And Call To Action	115

Dedication

I dedicate this book to all my teachers of education and of life, to my mentors, coaches, family, friends, colleagues, and clients who have so generously taught me so much about life and the human condition. They have shared their wisdom and knowledge with me, so I may learn and grow to be the grateful person I am today.

Now it is my time to share my lessons with others in the hope they too, may live their best life.

Introduction

This is a book about how to go about achieving your Big Hairy Audacious Goals in life, no matter what they may be for you.

Interwoven throughout the chapters of this book is information about how to achieve your wildest or deepest held dreams in life, along with examples from my own life experiences which have enabled me to achieve many of my life goals. I say *many* and not *all* of my life goals because I see setting goals, striving to achieve goals, then actually achieving those goals, then starting the process all over again, as the way to reach personal fulfillment, satisfaction, and happiness in life. I believe it is the best way to reach our fullest potential in any chosen endeavour we commit ourselves to undertake.

While I have achieved many goals in my life, I am always working towards achieving my next goal which, at the time of writing this book, is working on growing and building my own life and mindset coaching business which especially exists to support women to achieve in their lives. Why only women? Well, as a woman, I feel I have a depth of insight into the female experience. I love the men in my life. I am married to one and I have beautiful sons and grandsons who I love dearly, but I feel my expertise and experience of living a female life gives me a wealth of insight and understanding about the female condition which I can use to help other women.

I have worked in the women's community services for many years and provided support and help to hundreds of women who were escaping domestic violence and/or sexual assault. I have worked with women and taught women in higher education at university levels and I have a lot of experience from what I have learned in life about women, from my perspective as a woman. So my niche is to work with and support women to achieve their dreams and goals in life through the work I do with them in my life and mindset coaching business using the FIVE A's to Life Achievement Model which I have developed and is explained more fully within the chapters of this book.

I begin chapter one with looking at how I now run my coaching business, something that not so long ago I would never have imagined myself doing. Chapter two provides information about starting up a business and of the aspects that need to be thought of and incorporated to get set up and operating as a sole trader in business. Such a steep learning curve, but so rewarding and challenging, which I love. I am always up for a good challenge.

Following on from starting out, the next chapters provide information about finding the right coach for you and

Introduction

all the considerations that need to be thought of in this process. Seemingly, at every turn, there are elements of self-doubt that creep into our consciousness, which have to be quelled so we can keep moving forward to achieve our goals in life. The subconscious plays such an important role in how we think about ourselves and what we believe we are capable of, this is also explored within chapter four of the book.

Chapter five explores what goals are, big goals, little goals, everyday goals, SMART goals, and that one big goal which may be eluding you or it may have been sitting right there in the back of your mind, for years and years but you have never taken the steps to go after it. When you decide what you want to do and then you commit yourself to doing it, that's like finding that 'diamond in the rough' of life to go after. It can be exciting, exhilarating, and a little scary.

The latter chapters of the book look more closely at when the process works towards achieving your goals and the feelings of being totally in sync with whom you are when you work on this. There is a sense of being in the groove of total satisfaction when you are diligently and tenaciously working with your coach or mentor towards achieving your goals.

Negotiating the coaching relationship is important and is discussed in chapter seven of the book, as is acknowledging the highs and lows of the journey as you strive towards achieving your purpose. And, because of this, the importance of celebrating your achievements is reinforced and more importantly, to stop and celebrate along the way.

Big Hairy Audacious Goal

The acknowledgement that it is ok to think broadly and widely about future goals you set for yourself is covered in chapter nine, where it is recognised that changing lanes in life to take on a new goal which is completely left field for you, is perfectly acceptable and can be an exhilarating step in the journey of life.

The book reinforces in the last chapter that no matter what your goals are that successful people develop patterns of setting and then going after their dreams and goals and they never give up until they have reached that pinnacle for themselves. Then it is important to celebrate the wins and repeat the process.

I hope that reading the chapters of this book will raise for you thoughts about what it is you want to achieve in work or life. It will also provide you with the information you will need to enable you to know where to begin the process to find the right coach for you and what to expect when you work with a life and mindset coach.

I have written this book based on years of working with others to help them achieve their goals in life and it is my sincere desire to encourage and support as many people as I can in my lifetime, to go after their deepest held dreams and goals.

Be brave – do more, be more, and reach your dreams.
                                              Dr Anne Butcher

Chapter 1

How Did I End Up Here?

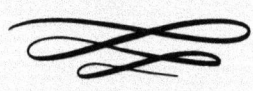

In 1995, when I graduated with a PhD in the discipline of Social Work from James Cook University in North Queensland, my husband and some of my closest friends, who knew my life story, urged me to write a book about it. Although flattered that anyone would think my life would interest others, I laughed it off and dismissed their encouragement, for the next fifteen years. However, a seed had been planted in my mind and from time to time over many years it kept emerging in my thoughts until I realised, for so many reasons, that I now wanted to write my life story. In fact, I felt compelled to do so for future generations, and especially for my immediate family.

In 2020, my first non-academic book was published. It was an exciting time as my dream had become a reality, and I held that book, my memoir, in my hands, almost in disbelief that I had actually done it! I'd written my story, and it was a very cathartic, almost therapeutic exercise to have done.

Writing that book opened a whole new world for me. Surprisingly, it launched me into establishing a whole new business career for myself. I like to think of it as my fourth career, and I am loving it. My earlier careers involved working for government, working in not for profit organisations, and working within family businesses, which I also loved. However, after over thirty years of working in front line, middle management, and then senior executive director roles, I tried retirement for a few months, but found it wasn't mentally stimulating enough for me. I had a lovely relaxing and refreshing break before I kick started my business for the very first time. It was simply registered as Dr Anne Butcher, so now I am relishing my life and my interests in my fourth career.

Big Hairy Audacious Goal

I saw an advertisement for a workshop in my hometown of Mackay, Queensland, Australia. It was a free workshop for anyone who had ever thought about writing a non-fiction book, so it immediately piqued my curiosity. I thought I would go along and check it out for myself to see what was involved. When I got there and listened to the unique strategies presented for getting a book written in a relatively short amount of time, it all seemed so achievable. I was hooked. My self-doubts and fears about writing my story melted away, and I could see how I could make this book become a reality. I signed up and over the next few months went on a journey of learning about book writing, the editing phases, graphic design, and book publishing processes which were all so different to anything I had ever done before and so very interesting to learn about.

Writing for academic journals and books was a very different process. I had published my doctoral thesis, but that was a matter of sending my thesis to the publishers and although they required some editing changes, it was pretty much published as written. This writing experience was different. I thoroughly enjoyed the freedom to write without the rigours of academic requirements impinging upon the process. I could just write my own thoughts freely and write in the first person as well. It was quite a liberating experience. I had many comments from those who have read my story about how readable that first book was, which is exactly how I intended it to be. So those comments were very much appreciated. I wrote my first book with Natasa Denman and her team at Ultimate 48 Hour Authors (U48A) publishing company. The same publishing company I have published this book with.

How Did I End Up Here?

They were brilliant at supporting me throughout both of my book writing processes.

I also learned that writing a book was not the end of the journey, it was just the beginning. Throughout the publishing process, they encouraged me to think of my book as being my 'business card on steroids'. I laughed when I first heard that phrase. I was assured my book would generate more opportunities for me, which it certainly has done in spades. I was encouraged to think of the book as the beginning of my new business, which took me a little while to get my head around, as I had not intended to create a new business for myself. I set out to write a book, that was it, just write a book. Now, I was being encouraged to see it as the entrée to a whole new business venture, something I had not even considered before I attended that workshop in Mackay.

As my book is a memoir, I asked myself how I could turn this book writing endeavour into a business. I knew my book was not going to do that. It would not make me rich. It was just something I felt I needed to do, but in the end, the idea came to me. It was that I had experienced adversity and triumph in my life, and along the way I had learnt many ways to overcome the challenges which life throws at all of us. I am a qualified social worker, so I had the skills, knowledge, and professional training to help others and it has always been my passion to do so. Therefore, the obvious conclusion for me was to use my life experiences and training to help, support, enable, motivate, encourage, inspire, mentor, and coach others on their life's journey.

Big Hairy Audacious Goal

I thought public speaking would be a good place to begin, particularly speaking to women's groups, as these were the logical cohorts who may feel motivated and inspired to take action in their own lives, and who may also connect with my own life story. Many women had told me how relatable my story was to their experience or to someone in their close circle of friends or family. I asked Natasa if she could recommend someone who could help me brush up on my public speaking skills. I was used to public speaking in my previous workforce and academic roles. But not in a way which would ensure it was informative, inspiring, motivating, humorous, warm, and engaging. Such as you would encounter at a dinner speaking event, as someone who may even entertain!

I knew I needed to learn new skills to engage with audiences in different settings, perhaps at social events or other special occasions. Natasa referred me to a colleague of hers, Janelle Johnston, who I engaged as my speaking coach. Meeting Janelle was a turning point for me as she coached me through her Empowered Speaker's program and then encouraged me to think more broadly about the business I could create for myself. I quickly realised that, with Janelle as my coach, I could learn how to create this business I had been thinking of, so I enrolled in her Business Breakthrough Mastery course to learn how to start up my own Life and Mindset Coaching Business. My entire career to this point had been as a social worker directly helping people or in management but always as an employee of either government or non-government services so I had never established a business of my own before, despite helping in other businesses operated by my family members. This was

How Did I End Up Here?

going to be entirely my business, and it was a new and exciting journey to be starting, albeit a little later in life but perfect in other ways, as I had all of that life experience and professional training to draw upon to help others to achieve their life goals. To me, it was a no brainer and a win/win situation both for me and for those with whom I would work in the future.

So, the beginning of my fourth career was set in motion and within the first year there was much learning to do about setting up and operating a business. I also brushed up on my skills by undertaking a couple of short courses to focus on mind and brain science to ensure my knowledge was current and at the cutting edge of the latest evidence-based research in this field of neuroscience. Upon completion of that program, I became a certified Neuro Change Practitioner. I am also an internationally certified life coach.

The cast had been set, and I was away into my new and exciting adventure.

Now, don't think I am someone who just thinks I am going to do something, then with 100% conviction, I just believe I can do it and get on with it. Oh no, there is a lot more than that for me and for just about everyone who thinks about taking on any new challenge in life. For me, this challenge came along at the right time, and I was ready to take another leap of faith in my life. I think the never ending and wonderful confidence that my husband has in me is way more than I sometimes have in myself, but he boosts my self-belief, so I find the courage to give new things a go. To me, it is about taking a calculated risk.

Big Hairy Audacious Goal

I weigh up all the pros and cons and the costs involved and what I hope to achieve and gain from taking on any new initiative. Now I was actually going to do what I ask my clients to do, and that is, to put their faith and trust in me to coach them to achieve their life dreams and goals. So, what kind of coach would I be if I didn't lead by my example?

I have always believed it is better to give something a go and fail than to die wondering if you could have made a success of yourself. Failure is a key ingredient to ultimately achieving success in life. If you don't fail, you don't learn what not to do in the future. Then when you try again, you shouldn't make the same mistakes. However, if you do, then you just get up, dust yourself off and start over again. So many well-known people in the world have done just that.

All these people have failed along their life's journey, but they got back up and started over again, learning from their failures along the way. People like, Steven Spielberg (award winning movie director), Stephen King (world renowned author), Michael Jordan (famous NBA player), JK Rowling (who wrote all the Harry Potter books and is the richest author in the world), Peter Thiel (founder of PayPal). Michael Jordan said, *'I've failed over and over and over again in my life and that is why I succeed'*.

Failures and mistakes provide us with important and necessary learning opportunities, which have the potential to propel us to succeed beyond our wildest dreams, just as it did for these famous people who initially failed spectacularly before going on to succeed spectacularly.

How Did I End Up Here?

We need to recognise these windows of opportunity when they occur, rather than solely wallowing in our own self-pity. Of course, wallowing is necessary, but it is important not to stay in that place for too long before you ask yourself, what can I learn from what just happened to me and how can I use this experience to my advantage as I start over again.

These are the messages of inspiration, hope, and motivation I use when working with my coaching clients. My coaching business has been operating for a couple of years and I have many coaching clients, all with their own unique goals, which they are working towards achieving. My coaching niche is to work with women who may be midlife or mid-career. They may be raising or have raised a family and they may have a little more time available to themselves now than ever before. These women are usually well educated and likely to still be working either full time or part time. What sets these women apart is they have always had a secret dream to do something just for themselves, and the thought of never fulfilling this dream causes them to have a feeling of general unhappiness or dissatisfaction in life. Like there is something more they need to do, or something is missing from their lives, which will bring them feelings of self fulfillment, achievement, satisfaction, and ultimately happiness.

This leaves them asking themselves, 'surely there has to be more in life than simply the work, home, work, never-ending cycle of life?'

Does this sound familiar to you? If so, what is your dream and what are you going to do to change this cycle, so you can have a much more fulfilling and purposeful life, doing what you *want* to do, not what you *have* to do?

For example, some women I have coached and worked with have had goals such as wanting to study at TAFE or university but they don't know where to begin, others want to do a PhD but need help to get into the system, others have wanted to start up their own consultancy business, while others have wanted to develop their self-confidence and self-belief, so they can achieve more at work and apply for that job up the next rung of the career ladder, or to simply have more confidence in dealing with other people at work and in life generally. These women want to get ahead, but they don't know how to or where to begin. I even have a client who I am coaching who wants to be a very senior politician in her country of origin and this is very achievable for her.

When I am working with these wonderful women, I sometimes pinch myself to know that I am fulfilling my own life goal, which is to train and coach other women to achieve in their lives. I am doing this while working for myself in my coaching business, working mostly from home, and earning a nice living for myself. I realise I am here because of the decisions I have made for myself, but I do still sometimes ask myself, almost in disbelief; how did I end up here?

'Life is what we make it, always has been, always will be.'

Grandma Moses

Chapter 2

Lights, Camera, Action!

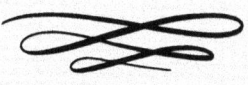

Oh, my goodness, this was really happening! I signed up with my business coach for twelve months and during that time, I need to think about all aspects of running a business to get set up and operating as soon as possible. It's all systems go!

As a social worker, we are not trained to think of ourselves as businesspeople because we usually are employed by an organisation to provide free services to people who are vulnerable or are in some type of difficult or challenging situation. This is what most social workers sign up for when they decide to study social work in the first place. Therefore, it is really quite a challenge to turn that thinking around and feel okay with offering life and mindset coaching services to women, and charge them a fee for doing so, even when I know and believe it will improve their lives.

During the year of working with my coach, whenever I sensed my self-doubts creeping in about what the heck I was doing, my coach was there to remind me of my focus and goals and the wealth of experience and knowledge I have gained over a lifetime of working, studying, and learning, which would benefit other people. She convinced me, if I did not provide coaching to others who wanted it, who would benefit from it, and were prepared to pay for it, I could potentially do them a disservice. So, I continued with my vision to support and coach others while also striving to create a viable business for myself.

I have spoken to other social workers who are also in private counselling practice or have run their own coaching businesses, and it is noticeable that we all

Big Hairy Audacious Goal

grapple with this wrenching of conscience regarding receiving payment for services. However, I sometimes think we are our own worst enemies as others in the helping professions such as psychologists, occupational therapists, speech therapists, physiotherapists etc. do not seem to have the same struggles of conscience. So why do we? It stems from the underpinning social justice principles of our profession, which believes in access, equity, fairness, and participation in society by all people, regardless of wealth, status, or position in society. However, as more and more social workers begin their own private practices, it is likely that working in business, knowing we are assisting people to improve the quality of their lives, will become more acceptable to those of us who choose to move towards becoming businesspeople as well as being social workers.

Together, my coach and I have worked through developing business plans and goals to get this new venture up and running. I would highly recommend to anyone who has a goal they want to achieve, to find themselves a coach or a mentor. No one ever achieves anything entirely on their own. Sure, you must do the legwork yourself, but there is always a need to have someone to talk ideas through with, to look at what the next steps are, to review with you how far you've come, and to hold you accountable for your own goals. Sounds crazy right? That someone should have to hold us accountable for achieving the goals that we set for ourselves, and we really want to achieve, but unless there is someone asking how you are going with the progress on those goals you set for yourself, it is too easy to think, I'll do that tomorrow or next week and before you know it a month has passed

Lights, Camera, Action!

by. We can all be the best procrastinators and at those times, never has the need to clean the house, or do the washing, or any of a million other jobs that we have put off for months or years, become more urgent than when we must sit down and apply ourselves to achieve our own goals.

The most successful people in life, regardless of their field of expertise, whether that be in business, sport, study, career etc. always have a mentor or a coach or some other important role model to help them achieve to their highest potential. They all need someone who can stretch their thinking and challenge them to see problems as opportunities and to think differently about how to solve those problems. They have had someone to show them the pathway to achieve their goals, and someone who has the experience and knowledge to add a depth of thinking and new perspectives to discussions, to find the next steps forward, while also holding them accountable along the way. Sounds hard, but it works!

The practical steps of starting up my business had to be done, so I registered the business with the Australian Securities Investment Commission (ASIC), had my website created, set up all the social media sites I needed to operate a business. I contracted people who had expertise in social media and graphic arts to look after these aspects of business, as they are not my strength areas and before too long, they were created and on my social media platforms. Obviously, I needed to have input into the development and shaping of the branding and the image I wanted to create for myself, as impressions are everything, but I am happy with the end results and

Big Hairy Audacious Goal

the belief they will also appeal to my target audience. I also employed a casual bookkeeper to help me set up my financial record keeping systems and train me in how to use these tools for myself, so I can keep these records maintained and up to date.

I developed content materials to run online webinars which were focused on helping people to start thinking about whether they had a big life goal they wanted to achieve. Some people know immediately when I speak to them about what their big life goal is, that one thing they must do before they die, whether that be travel or getting a better job or having a complete change of life and work balance, or mending relationships with family or friends, or studying or any of a million other possibilities that it could be.

While reading this, did a thought pop into your head about your big life goal? Have you ever thought about this? Did you know what it was in an instant, or do you not know exactly what that might be yet, but you do have a feeling that you are meant to be doing something more with your life, you're meant to achieve something else, but you haven't pinned it down to exactly what that is just yet?

I have met so many people who have told me this is exactly what they feel at certain times in their life. If that feeling doesn't go away, you can take it as a sign that you need to be doing something else and life is too short to not get started on working out what that is for you. Your big goal should both excite you and scare you, otherwise you are not dreaming big enough. It needs to be realistic and achievable as well, but most of us think too small

Lights, Camera, Action!

because thinking big is scary. I want to say to you, think scary, find the right coach, or mentor for you, and go for it.

Write down here the top 1 to 3 goals you want to achieve in your life while you can. This is just for you so imagine if there were no barriers to achieving your big goal, no financial constraints, no one telling you that you can't or shouldn't do something and you had all the skills training and knowledge you needed to achieve your goal. Nothing is there to hold you back, so what would your big goal or goals be? Write them here.

1. _____

2. _____

3. _____

Now you have identified your big goal. What are you going to do to set about achieving it for yourself?

You don't want to be that one old person in the nursing home looking back on your life and thinking,

'if only I had done *(insert your dream here)* when I could have.'

That is the yardstick I use for myself. If ever I am unsure about whether to take on a new goal for myself, like starting up my own business, I ask myself,

'if I don't do this, will I regret it?'

Big Hairy Audacious Goal

If the answer is yes, then I know I must do it. Hence, the life and mindset coaching business is set up and I am achieving more than I could have ever thought possible. I have a big dream about where I want to take this business and I am on a mission to turn it into a hugely successful business so not only can I earn a living, but it will give me great satisfaction knowing how many people I have been able to coach on their life's journey as well. I will be the little old lady in the nursing home, in the rocking chair in the corner, feeling happy and satisfied that I didn't leave anything undone that I really wanted to do in my life.

Going back to the business side of things, I realised there was a lot of money going out in set up costs and training and coaching for myself, but not much coming back in. I knew I needed to get some returns on my investment and do something more to generate an income if this business was to become financially viable, while also holding true to my goals of wanting to support and help others to achieve their life goals. I thought about what I could do in the short term to generate an income while I was setting up and running my webinars and coaching business.

I decided to incorporate into my business a private social work counselling practice for two days each week. I knew there was a need for counselling support for people with mental health concerns, more so now than ever before, given the impact of the COVID-19 pandemic upon us all. The stressors of everyday life significantly affected many people in these unprecedented times we are all living through.

Lights, Camera, Action!

To establish a private counselling practice, I needed a suitable counselling space. I soon located and hired a perfect room to use. I registered myself as a private practitioner with local providers who soon began referring clients to me. I really enjoy being able to counsel and support people who are going through complex life problems and seeing many of them make good progress to cope better in their lives is very satisfying for me. It has been a very rewarding experience and is very complimentary to the life and mindset coaching side of my business.

I want to ensure I am clear here, that counselling is not coaching, and coaching is not counselling. There is quite a different focus when providing therapeutic counselling services to an individual than when working as a life and mindset coach to get the best out of the client so they can go on to achieve a very specific goal in their life.

While the counselling practice became operational quickly, because of the high level of need in the community, I was simultaneously, advertising free online webinars on all the usual social media platforms, to hold free events for anyone interested in achieving something more for themselves in life and to attract coaching clients. I have run many webinars and had so many women attending and interested in achieving a dream they have. I have also had women who are looking for someone to help them define and answer the question they ask of themselves, *what more is there in life for me?*

I set myself a quota to achieve the number of coaching clients that I could comfortably manage in a one-on-one setting while also ensuring my clients were getting their goals met. I have also set up online courses and programs which my clients can continue to work on in a self-paced mode which is less intensive for them and for me and allows for an up-scaling of the business over time.

I have tried some activities along the way which have not yielded any good leads in terms of new clients, but they have been fabulous learning experiences for me such as attending a Women in Business Expo on the Gold Coast. That was a fun experience, and I met some wonderful women running their own businesses there. I managed to get some follow up work from the expo, which was unexpected. It related to funding and grant writing for another business owner who wanted to submit a research and development grant application for her business. My decades of working in government and the not-for-profit sector have provided me with a wealth of experience in this area, either as a grant and tender writer myself, or being on panels which assess grant applications. It is another string to my bow which came up in discussion at the women's expo and they asked me to assist with a research and development grant application, which I was happy to do. Sometimes opportunities come along in the most unexpected places and times, but I have found keeping an open mind to whatever may come along has helped me to take advantage of those opportunities. Mindset plays a key role in whatever you do and it is so critical to success to maintain an open mindset to consider all possibilities which may come your way.

There is one tip which I would like to share, to ensure you are not disappointed in your own ventures. It is to prepare yourself mentally for all outcomes of whatever you take on. This is how I prepare myself for disappointments, because when you prepare mentally for the worst outcome, if it should happen, you are not really all that disappointed as you have thought about it beforehand and have at least prepared yourself a little. Then you can take on the challenge, knowing what the worst possible outcome could be and having put some thought into that. Therefore, should it happen, it is not a surprise, and you learn from it, or take from it what you will, such as making new business contacts and creating brand awareness, then move onto your next challenge.

I use this approach in all areas of my work and personal life. Just ask yourself, what is the worst that can happen, and if your response to yourself is something you absolutely cannot live with, then the risk is too high, and you probably shouldn't take it on. However, if you can live with the disappointment of that worst case scenario you have thought of and you can turn your attention to focusing on it being a positive learning, growth experience, for the future, then all is not lost.

I love this quote by **Adrianna Huffington**, which I think says it all for me regarding this topic.

> **'Failure is not the opposite of success. It's part of success.'**

If we never fail, we will not learn what doesn't work and therefore, what will work.

Chapter 3
Finding Your Sensei

In life, we meet many people in various contexts such as at school, at work, in sporting groups, in religious groups, at university, while volunteering etc. and in so many more settings. Sometimes we meet people to whom we seem automatically drawn. We feel a connection with them in a short space of time. We soon come to realise there is an affinity between us both. These are people whose company we enjoy being in and we seem to get on well with, right from the start. It is at these times you may have noticed that you just feel aligned with that other person. In truth, you probably have similar values and beliefs about aspects of life, family, and society. You may share similar worldviews, even if you come from vastly diverse backgrounds. There just seems to be a synergy that works between you both.

I know I have met many people in my lifetime and this synergy I am referring to just seems to be there between us right from the get-go. It seems like we have both known each other for years, except we haven't. We can talk about any number of topics for ages. The conversation flows freely and easily between us and there is a feeling of general congruence with how we view the world. On those occasions, when this happens, I know I have felt quite exhilarated afterwards and amazed at how easily the connection between us had occurred.

One example of this occurring relates to a woman much younger than me. We arranged to meet for a work meeting at a coffee shop. When we met, we talked about the usual introductory comments about our work, but before we talked about the work purpose of the meeting, the conversation had moved to sharing information about each other and our backgrounds and family members and before we knew it, this synergy was occurring. We identified a lot of similarities in our backgrounds, which was quite surprising to us both. After talking about the original work-related purpose of the meeting, and as I was about to leave the job that brought me to that meeting in the first place, we agreed to keep in touch with each other. We have done so now for many years. It has opened opportunities for us both where we have collaborated on shared pieces of work together. We planned to co-write a book together, and I was even invited to be the guest speaker at the International Women's Day event hosted by her employer. We never know where friendships and opportunities may come from, but we need to be open to embracing them when they come along, as sometimes amazing and unexpected experiences present themselves to us on our life's journey.

The reason for raising these synergies between people is to create awareness about noticing when these connections present themselves to us. They are important to notice as they often present openings to collaborate on tasks and projects together, which can be mutually beneficial. It is important to look for these types of compatibilities and synergies when seeking a mentor or coach to work with. Not only do you need to have confidence in your coach and a belief in their knowledge, skills, experience, and abilities to take you to another level of self-development, but they also must be people who you have a certain values alignment or synergy with. It is essential that you know, like, and trust each other. I am so fortunate that my coach, Janelle Johnston, has been the perfect match for me. She has guided and challenged me when needed, while also reassuring me and teaching me important aspects of my new business venture. It has been and remains a great match between us. She is the perfect sensei for me.

For any relationship to work, whether that be work related or in your personal life, there must be a level of trust and confidence in the other person. It is in this trust that you will allow yourself to lower your guard and be vulnerable enough to expose your inner thoughts and feelings, and genuinely listen to the comments and feedback from the coach about these areas and many other aspects of yourself which may be hard to hear at times, but it is important to listen and consider the feedback being gifted to us. Yes, I said gifted as I see these times of honest feedback, given with good intent as gifts to help us develop and mature our insightfulness about ourselves. This is how we learn and grow, and it needs to be seen and accepted as a gift to us, to be taken without defensiveness or hurt feelings being allowed to enter that moment.

We need to be open to accept constructive feedback, even if that is sometimes difficult to hear about ourselves. Our inner strength and growth comes from having an open mind and, at the very least, to consider feedback, which should stretch and challenge us, otherwise we will not improve and develop in the areas we need to if we want to succeed and achieve our goals.

We can become defensive, and we can become angry or even upset when hearing constructive feedback, but in doing so, our minds are closed off to truly hearing information which highlights the areas, we need to work on to stretch us enough to achieve our goals. We have choices to make to either be brave enough to listen to and consider constructive, but possibly confronting, feedback about ourselves, or be closed off and feel wounded anyone would say such things to us. Alternatively, we can take the comments on board, consider them, and look at what we can learn from them and then take from them what we will. The choice is ours to make. We can either accept some or all of the feedback or we can reject it entirely. The critical lesson here is to at least consider the feedback before rejecting some or all of it.

As a life and mindset coach it is so important for the person I am coaching to feel comfortable enough with me and trust me enough to allow themselves to be vulnerable, to ask questions which they may think are stupid or they should already know, but don't, and to open themselves up to consider new information and new ways of thinking, working or living and placing their vulnerabilities in the hands of their coach. Unless we can do this with the coach we are working with, we will not truly benefit from and get the most out of the coaching relationship.

It is so important to get the right person when looking for a coach. It is okay to try out one or two coaches until you find the right coach for you. Someone who you believe is the right fit for you. It is in finding the right coach that you will benefit most from the coaching relationship and that is what we all want from our coach, isn't it? And that is what we are paying them for, otherwise, what is the point of being coached?

Finding Your Sensei

The second most important aspect of having a successful coaching relationship is to realise that a coach can only do so much. They may have the most experience and knowledge of any coach you could have in the areas which you want to develop in. They may be the perfect match for you in terms of compatibility and knowing how to get the best out of you to achieve the goals you have set for yourself. This is the ideal situation. However, it will count for nothing unless you, as the person being coached, take full responsibility for your own learning and development. It is like the old saying *'you can take a horse to water, but you can't make it drin*k'. Similarly, a coach can be the best person with the best skills, experience, knowledge and abilities and they can show you the steps to take to achieve your big dream or goals in life or career, but they cannot do the work for you. Only you can do that for yourself. You need to fully commit to achieving the goal you have set for yourself to get the most out of the coaching relationship and experience.

Many times, I have heard others talk about coaches they have worked with and made comments such as, 'they were not a good coach', and I wonder, whether they *really* are not a good coach, or was it you who didn't follow through on the steps you needed to take, to achieve your goals. No one achieves anything in life unless they take responsibility for themselves and their own actions. I have worked with many people in many settings in my thirty plus year career and have heard so many people say they hadn't achieved a particular goal because it was someone else's fault. When working in child protection and youth justice in particular, I could give countless examples of parents or young people when asked why they didn't attend court or a probation meeting or countless other important appointments and the response is that someone else didn't arrange a lift for them, or didn't wake them up in time, or they forgot, or anyone of a million other excuses. However, what it ultimately boils down to is they did not take responsibility for themselves and make those appointments a priority in their life. It is always easier to blame someone else than accept they messed up.

When I hear someone apportioning blame to others for their own actions or inactions, I immediately wonder if that is the usual default position for that person, that whenever anything does not work out for them, no matter what that may be, whether it is always someone else's fault. Do they ever take responsibility for themselves?

It is in the taking of responsibility for ourselves that we learn where we need to improve and develop further. We see where we have areas to work on and master, which will build a platform for us to develop to the next level. This provides us with an opportunity to continuously improve ourselves, a learning experience which we must take, use, learn from and make changes within ourselves to develop, grow, improve, and become the best version of ourselves. This is what Abraham Maslow called 'self-actualisation' and is defined by Wikipedia as '… the highest level of psychological development where personal potential is fully realized after basic bodily and ego needs have been fulfilled.'

So do not be afraid to find the right coach for you, the right teacher, the right sensei. Arrange to have a conversation

Finding Your Sensei

with a couple of coaches to make sure you find the right one for you. It is important they are a coach who you feel most aligned to and comfortable with. The person who you feel you can trust and feel safe enough to allow them to see who you really are, with all your vulnerabilities, flaws and weaknesses, and someone you are comfortable to share your deepest dreams and goals with. When you find the right coach and you work with them to develop your plan to achieve your goals and think of their constructive feedback as a gift to you. Then you will soar ahead to achieve your goal in life.

> *'If you reject feedback, you also reject the choice of acting in a way that may bring you abundant success.'*
> **John Matt**

Chapter 4

Slaying The Dragon

In my younger year's I was always intrigued by Henry Ford's famous saying:

> **'Whether you think you can, or you think you can't – you're right.'**

I mean, how can they both be right? At first glance, it doesn't make sense, does it?

It wasn't until years later, after a lot of study and life experiences, that I have come to fully understand just how correct each of these statements are. So much depends upon whichever one you believe of yourself in any situation, and can determine your whole life experience and future outcomes. It really is that profound.

Let me explain. Whether I am working with my coaching clients or in my private counselling practice, so much of the focus of my approach is informed by how the person I am working with or coaching sees themselves and believes in themselves.

So, what is a belief exactly? According to the Neuro Change Institute (2021):

> **'It is an attitude or a conviction about the truth of some idea or concept.'**

Where do our beliefs come from? As children, we usually grow up within our own family, with our parents, who are the first and most influential force in shaping our beliefs right from birth, or at least as soon as we can start to remember and mimic behaviours and words. We are taught right from wrong, good from bad, what to do in certain situations and what not to do in others. We watch and listen to our parents and extended family members, and we see their actions and hear their comments and views about all manner of things in the family, the neighbourhood, the community, or in the world more broadly from news events on the television, radio, social media etc. Our views and our beliefs are all being shaped during these times by all these influences around us, without us even being conscious of it.

These beliefs are further shaped by our peer groups, our teachers at school, sporting teams and groups, coaches, church groups, employment experiences or any of the many other significant groups we may become involved in as we grow into adulthood. These beliefs become cumulative, and we may not even be conscious of them, but they become our truth and what we believe. These are the beliefs we live by, stand up for, argue for, fight for, die for, and hold dear as the core nucleus of our very being and who we are. They are the unconscious beliefs that make up our worldview and our view of ourselves and others within it. They form the basis of our judgements of self and others. They are a very powerful force in our life. In the world of psychology, these are called 'dispositional' beliefs because they form our basic predispositions as human beings towards our inner self as well as everything external to ourselves.

These dispositional beliefs may work well for us if the messages we received about ourselves from our parents, other individuals, groups, and living environments were predominantly positive and we grew up to believe that we

Dedication

are strong, confident, capable, and can do anything we put our minds to types of messages, then usually, this is what we grow up believing of ourselves. Generally, this works well for us. However, the converse is also true. If the messages we grew up with about ourselves were that, we are not good enough in many areas of our lives, that we would not amount to anything, that we could not or should not expect too much of ourselves because of our gender, or sexuality, or ethnicity, or our abilities, or our intellect, then it is highly likely that we grew up believing these views of ourselves too. These self-perceptions can have such a detrimental effect on people and are the cause of why so many people are in therapy or have mental health problems, or use self-harming behaviours, because in their minds and belief systems, they are unconsciously saturated with the messages that they are not good enough and they never will be. This is when people find they cannot cope with life which often leads them to turn to negative coping mechanisms such as substance abuse (drugs and alcohol) which aids in removing them from the pain and reality of everyday life, or they remove themselves from life all together, sadly, through suicide.

The messaging we receive from significant people in our lives is just so important, right from birth. However, when this doesn't happen, all is not lost, as humans do have the amazing ability to change their beliefs and to learn and grow and create a new identity through psychosocial education, and awareness raising, and cognitive behaviour therapies.

If we never stop to question our beliefs, then we will go through life with unconscious biases towards those dispositional beliefs we grew up with, which may or may not be serving us well in life. If you examine your own life views:

- Are you on top of your game and living your best life?
- Or are you not where you would hope to be at your current age and stage in life?
- And, if so, how are you managing your feelings of disappointment?
- What positive or negative coping methods are you drawn to use to get through each day, week, month, and year?
- Do you need to change anything or are you happy with your own self beliefs?

Usually, during adolescence, when a young person's individual identity is being formed, it is a time of exploration and reflection of inner beliefs instilled within us from childhood. At this time of life, a young person will likely either reinforce their identity through embracing the beliefs they have been brought up to believe, or they may reject some or all of them completely. This is when adolescents are seen to be rebellious. When they seem to go in a completely different direction to the one they were brought up in. Adolescence is such a powerful time in a young person's life, and it is usually the time for teenagers to work out who they are, where they fit into society, and within their families, and determine what they truly believe. This is when they either strongly accept, or clearly reject, long held beliefs and biases imbued by osmosis throughout their childhood.

Dedication

I believe an exercise of deep reflection on what our dispositional beliefs are is crucial for a person to grow and develop into the mature, informed, thinking person they may wish to become. This is a process of examining, in depth, those beliefs which were previously just accepted, without much thought, *just because we always have.* We then make decisions about which of these beliefs we choose to continue to hold true to and therefore, make conscious decisions to keep, as opposed to those which we come to realise we no longer believe in, but we have been living by them *just because we always have.* To go through this process of deep self-reflection, self-examination, and questioning of oneself is a truly cathartic and important developmental growth experience which some people undergo as they mature.

When we make a conscious decision to embrace those beliefs which we know are now our truth, and we re-commit to them, these then are reinforced as our core beliefs.

Many years ago, I went through this process myself and I came out of that experience, realising I was simply unconsciously accepting the Catholic religious faith that my parents had brought me up in. It had been reinforced through my family, my schooling, and the church I attended as a child. After much reflection and introspection, I decided I did not, in fact, believe in God or the afterlife and I had been going through the motions of attending church, simply because that was what was expected of me. However, after going through this deep introspective process of consciousness raising about my own beliefs and then intentionally deciding which of these I chose to continue to accept, or reject entirely, I realised I didn't believe in these things any longer at all. I weened myself off church gradually and now my core belief, which sits quite comfortably with me, is that I am atheist.

Some people seem to go through life without ever questioning their dispositional beliefs and consciously deciding on and accepting what their core beliefs are and this amazes me. I do not advocate for what anyone should or shouldn't believe. That is for them to work out and decide upon for themselves. However, I think an essential element of continuous human growth and development, psychologically and emotionally, requires an examination of dispositional beliefs and then a conscious determination of, and recommitment to, those we choose to retain as our core beliefs and a letting go of those we do not wish to keep any longer. This is a type of intentionally slaying those belief dragons which do not serve us.

Undertaking this process requires honesty, through deep reflection and introspection, and it is not to say that this process cannot be undertaken and repeated at various stages of life and self-development. It is not as though once we have done this, that is a process never undertaken again. Quite the contrary, at various points throughout the lifespan, it is almost inevitable that this reflective process will re-occur and if we maintain an open mindset in life, then it is important to take the opportunity, when it does arise to review your own beliefs and ask yourself:

Dedication

- Do I still believe in ….?
    If yes, then ask yourself -
- Why do I still believe in that?
    If the answer is no, then it is equally important to ask yourself -
- What has changed and why don't I believe that anymore?
- What do I now believe instead?

There is no right or wrong answer to these questions, so long as it is not hurting yourself or anyone else or breaking the law, it is just a process of reflection and re-determination of who you are as a person at any given point in your lifetime.

The most positive message I hope you are taking from this chapter is that beliefs can be changed if they are not serving us well in our life or if they are holding us back from achieving our dreams and goals. It takes time, perseverance, and consistency in working towards changing a long-held belief, but the good news is, it can be done if you want to do so. If you don't know how, or where, to begin then I suggest finding yourself a life and mindset coach to work with to develop new beliefs which can open new doors and opportunities which you could probably never have imagined before, particularly if you have always had it reinforced to you that you would not, or could not, ever expect to be more than you already are in life. This is not true, and I am here to tell you – you can be! You just need to believe you can.

There is the matter of understanding the differences between what is our will compared to what is our belief.

Big Hairy Audacious Goal

You might have the will (desire) to change, but if you don't believe you can, then you will never change. For example, how many of us have had the will to go to the gym, to get fit, to lose a few kilograms? We usually start off great because we want to do it. We are motivated, and we have the will to succeed. However, if we believe we will probably lose weight but then put it all back on, like we did last time, then sure enough that is what will happen because when there is a contest between the will and beliefs - beliefs will win every time.

Therefore, it is so important to believe that you can achieve that big hairy audacious goal that you dare dream of for yourself, because if you do, it can happen. You will find a way to make it happen. In fact, that's the only way humankind has ever achieved anything of note. Just as when John F. Kennedy said in 1961 that the Americans would put a man on the moon, imagine what everyone must have thought of such an unbelievable goal when that momentous announcement was made at the time. However, those working on this project and the USA government believed they could do it and they wanted to beat the Soviet Union in that space race, which provided the focus and determination to succeed. Eight years later, it became a reality when Neil Armstrong was the first person ever to set foot on the moon. This is a powerful demonstration of self-belief to achieve an unimaginable goal, but they did it.

> *'You don't become what you want, you become what you believe.'*
>
> **Oprah Winfrey**

Chapter 5

Diamonds In The Rough

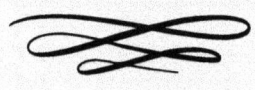

A very important element to achieve success in life is to know and be clear about what your purpose is. Purpose is your reason for being, what defines your authentic self at your core, what motivates you to get up in the morning and for doing everything you do in life with enthusiasm and energy with a vision of what you are striving to achieve, so it doesn't seem like hard work at all.

Your purpose, when you are clear about it and tenaciously embrace it, can motivate and drive you to set goals and steadfastly work towards achieving them, never giving up until you succeed. When I talk about goals, I would like to be clear that there are goals at all levels. Every one of us sets goals every day. We might have the goal to get to work on time, or the goal to pick up some groceries on the way home, or the goal to organise your child's birthday party or attend some special event for yourself. These are everyday goals which most of us don't think much about at all. We probably don't recognise these as goals but simply things we need to do each day to run our lives and that of our family. We just get on with them and do what we need to do. These small goals are necessary and important to maintaining a healthy functioning life, whereby you participate in your family, your work, your community, and within society.

In this chapter, I am focusing on those big and exciting goals that most people only ever dream of. They are the thoughts that flash across our mind when we allow ourselves to dream and to think, *If only I could do/be/have/go to*

Big Hairy Audacious Goal

Take a minute here to think about what your big dream is. What would you insert in this space? Have you got a big dream or goal? Something you would love to do and maybe have been thinking about for many years? Something that really excites you when you think of it. Or are you someone who can't really pin that big goal down for yourself just yet, but you have a feeling there is more you should do with your life and that thought just stays with you for months or even years? It stays with you while you keep going through the mundane, routine, motions of your everyday life and work cycle, while never really feeling fulfilled and being conscious that the clock of life keeps ticking, while you still haven't worked out what is your big goal. This can generate feelings of general unhappiness and dissatisfaction with life. Take note if this is how you feel, as it is an indication that maybe you are not doing what you truly would like to be doing.

Not everyone has a clear purpose or goal to work towards and many people don't know where to begin to work out what their purpose in life is. Therefore, many people are constantly searching for meaning and purpose in their lives. They usually ask themselves questions from time to time, such as:

- What is my life all about?
- What am I doing?
- What am I meant to be doing?
- What else could I, or should I be doing?

Does this sound like you? If so, there are coaches and personal development professionals who can help you work this out. You just need to find one that is the right match for you.

There are many more questions we ask ourselves, all with the same objective of trying to figure out what gives our life meaning, other than our families and loved ones of course, our reason for living, and what we put our energy into every day. When we find it, it is like finding a diamond in the rough in our lives because our purpose aligns with our flow in life, as though the two meld together. When this happens, you can find yourself in the moment of working toward your goals and it is like time stands still. Have you ever been so engrossed in what you are doing that hours fly by without you even noticing it, or been conscious of the time that has elapsed at all? When you're in this state of purpose and flow people, forget to eat or sleep, as they are so enthralled, immersed, and enlivened by what they are doing. It is truly like nothing else matters at all during these times.

Many fortunate people have found their purpose through their family and important relationships or through a special interest area they have, or their faith or vocation of some type, or in their work or profession or their day-to-day work, life. Other people just seem to have a feeling that what they are doing is not a good fit for them and there is something else they could or should do which would bring much more meaning and purpose for them to engage in. Others have managed to turn their passion into their life's focus and have created an income stream for themselves in doing so. You've no doubt heard the saying.

Big Hairy Audacious Goal

'If you turn your passion into your obsession, you will never work a day in your life again'. This is, of course, the ultimate goal.

Then there are others who seek tree changes or sea changes and sometimes they do find what it is they are looking for such as moving from the corporate world to become a farmer or moving from the rural areas to start up a new life and career in a metropolitan area. For many who make these significant life changes, it seems everything just feels right to them, and they have found their purpose and fit in life, which can be immensely satisfying and almost cathartic for them.

For those who are still trying to optimistically investigate this for themselves, I say keep searching because you will eventually find your way to what it is you are meant to be doing. It doesn't have to be something you do on your own. In most instances, you will need someone who is experienced, objective, and removed from the emotions of your life to assist you to work this out. It may mean taking a leap of faith and initially jumping into areas you think maybe what you want to focus on. However, you may find they are not for you in the end. If you don't give these ideas a go, you will always be wondering if you should have done so. Also, trying out something new brings with it new learnings and opportunities which can and often does, lead into totally unexpected valuable learning experiences and new opportunities.

Amazingly, there are also people who never seem to question or seek their purpose in life in the first place, or they have given up on their quest to find these answers for themselves all together. This can have devastating consequences, as they often seek destructive means to cope with a desolate sense of hopelessness in life. I have worked with thousands of people over the years for whom a sense of hopelessness or chaos is their normal and most have had traumatic life experiences as well. I do not judge them as I have not walked in their shoes, but, I encourage them to seek the help and support of people who are skilled enough to help them find a purpose in life as this is the only thing that has the potential to help them turn their lives around for the better.

Conversely, there are others who have been fortunate enough to have figured out their life goal. They have developed their sense of life's purpose and focus. These people are very clear about what it is they are striving to achieve and, more importantly, why they are doing what they do every day. They approach every day with clarity, focus, and drive. They have a clear plan, either written down as a visual motivational tool, or in their mind's eye. These plans set out how they are going to achieve their goal, or where they are at any given time, in the process of achieving it.

Having such a clear focus and reaching important milestones along the way can instil a sense of fulfillment, achievement, and satisfaction, which all enhance personal mental health and wellbeing through positivity and optimism. These benefits come from living life with purpose and meaning.

Some goals may take a short time to achieve, such as applying for a job and being fortunate enough to land it straight up. Other goals may take a little longer, like losing weight, or training to run a marathon, or working on improving family relationships, or saving a deposit for your first house, or planning an overseas trip, etc. The possibilities are endless. Other goals may take many years to achieve, such as completing a university degree or climbing up the career ladder to reach the top of your profession, or paying off your mortgage, or becoming the top sports person you want to be or any number of a million other possibilities which a life goal could be.

If you take a moment to think about any goal you have ever set for yourself, which you worked on achieving, diligently and consistently, with drive and motivation to achieve, you will know exactly what I am talking about. The health and wellbeing benefits which flow from having a positive purpose in life, of developing your own plan about how you are going to achieve it, while remaining focused and clear about your own self-belief to achieve your goals, are significant and well documented. Research has shown that an optimistic attitude with positive thoughts release neuropeptides which help to fight stress and a range of potentially more serious illnesses (Dweck, 2008).

I need to also add that purpose in life usually changes at various times throughout the lifespan. So, when we are younger, our goals may be to get a car, or find a job, or find a partner, or rent our first unit or place to live. Then, as we age, our purpose may change to become more about settling down, having a family, buying a house, etc. At various times throughout the stages of life, your goals are likely to change, just as your needs and those of your family are changing as well.

Diamonds In The Rough

There are, of course, some people who never consciously strive to achieve a particular purpose or goal in life. They simply seem to float through life and take each day as it comes. These people operate on a sleep, work, eat, repeat type of mindset and nothing much changes in their lives. Some people appear to be content with this laissez-faire lifestyle and good luck to them if they are happy in themselves. It may be a very stress-free way to live, but they will never move from where they are in life to achieve more than they already have. Is this a negative thing? Maybe not, only those who live in this domain can answer that question. Then, there are others who constantly strive to achieve their purpose and, in doing so they set clear life goals to attain for themselves. Therefore, they tend to be life's higher achievers.

One thing I have learned throughout my career and my life generally, is that people who set themselves goals and have a clear purpose for why they want to reach those goals, achieve success in their life, often to a greater level than they could have ever anticipated. This is because striving to achieve anything creates new learnings and brings us into contact with other people and when this occurs, inevitably, opportunities open for us, which we could never have foreseen. Opportunities such as completely new life experiences, unanticipated travel, new paying work offers, collaborations with others on projects, and many other possibilities that may present themselves. The important point here, is to remain open-minded to at least consider new possibilities when they are offered to you, as they can sometimes be a little left field and not something you might ever have imagined seeing yourself do, but taking a chance on

Big Hairy Audacious Goal

doing something completely different can also put you into direct contact with people you would probably never have met in your usual social or work circles. This has the potential to create new possibilities and opportunities. Networking is critical to relationship development and the creation of possibilities which could never have been imagined previously. These are the things that make life so interesting and exciting because there is an element of risk attached to doing something completely different. If you enter any opportunity having considered all possible risks and you're still prepared to give it a go, you will be pleasantly surprised at what may unfold for you in life.

I have developed these steps to follow to get started on achieving your success in life. As I list them below, ask yourself, how would I answer each of these?

1. Set yourself a goal and make it a **SMART** goal (it must be **S**pecific, **M**easurable, **A**chievable, **R**ealistic (so it can't be to win lotto), and it should be achievable in a **T**imely manner. The flowchart on the following page will assist you in developing your own SMART goal.

2. If you know the steps to take to achieve your goal, then map them out using the Smart Goal Flow Chart included (on next page).

3. If you don't know the steps to take to achieve your goal, then start searching by asking people you know and trust who they may recommend to you, or find yourself a mentor or life coach to get you started on the journey. This may of course

depend on what your goal is and how significant that goal may be for you as to who you choose to approach.

4. Remember, if the goal is a huge life goal for you but one which you dream of, it should excite you when you think of it, and it should also bring about a feeling of fear because it's something you want so badly in life.

5. If this is the case, then invest in yourself. Put your money into the development of yourself. If you need to find a coach who can get you started on the journey to achieve that goal or stay with you throughout the journey, then it is an investment in your future. It is not selfish to invest in yourself, as this is how success is attained. It is the same action taken by elite sports people to reach the pinnacle of their sport.

6. When you achieve each goal, it is so important to stop and take time out to acknowledge the hard work taken to achieve the goal, then celebrate the attainment of your goal and take a little time out to have a rest and regroup while you consider what the next goal will be for you to begin working on.

7. Set your next goal or write a list of goals you want to achieve. Choose the next most important goal for you, then start the process all over again to work towards achieving your dreams. Other than winning lotto or receiving an inheritance, this is the only legal way to get ahead in life.

SMART Goals

Big Hairy Audacious Goal

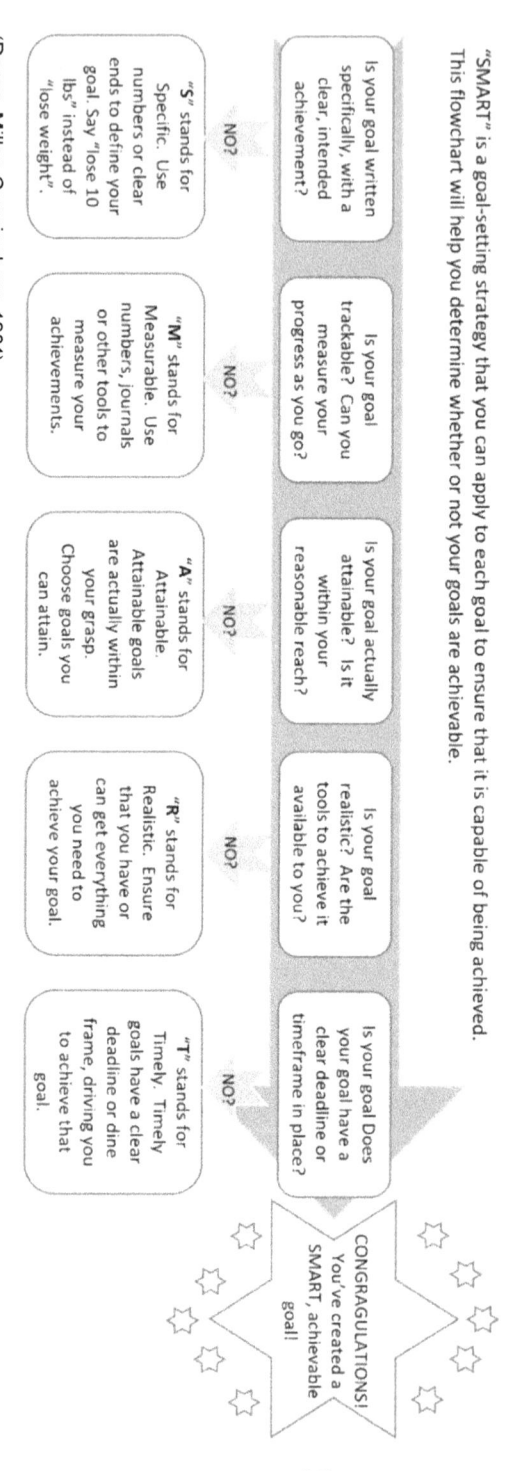

"SMART" is a goal-setting strategy that you can apply to each goal to ensure that it is capable of being achieved. This flowchart will help you determine whether or not your goals are achievable.

- Is your goal written specifically, with a clear, intended achievement?
  - NO? → "S" stands for Specific. Use numbers or clear ends to define your goal. Say "lose 10 lbs" instead of "lose weight".
- Is your goal trackable? Can you measure your progress as you go?
  - NO? → "M" stands for Measurable. Use numbers, journals or other tools to measure your achievements.
- Is your goal actually attainable? Is it within your reasonable reach?
  - NO? → "A" stands for Attainable. Attainable goals are actually within your grasp. Choose goals you can attain.
- Is your goal realistic? Are the tools to achieve it available to you?
  - NO? → "R" stands for Realistic. Ensure that you have or can get everything you need to achieve your goal.
- Is your goal Does your goal have a clear deadline or timeframe in place?
  - NO? → "T" stands for Timely. Timely goals have a clear deadline or dine frame, driving you to achieve that goal.

CONGRAGULATIONS! You've created a SMART, achievable goal!

(Doran, Miller, Cunningham; 1981)

Diamonds In The Rough

After completing your SMART GOAL flow chart and you know, or at least have a good idea, about what goal or goals you want to achieve to fulfill your purpose in life. What's the next step for you? Are you going to close this chapter of this book after having read this information and do nothing more, or are you going to take action to do something about it? The choice is yours to make, but my advice to you is - if you don't know where to start, talk to a life coach.

> *'Life isn't about finding yourself. Life is about creating yourself'.*
> **George Bernard Shaw**

Chapter 6

In The Groove

Let's imagine you have identified your purpose or goal in life. It is sitting there, in your mind, you clearly know what it is you want to do and what benefits it will bring to you and those closest to you in your life once you have achieved it… but how do you do this? Where do you start? How do you get from point A to point Z in your life, to claim that elusive prize and fully realise that exciting purpose you have for yourself? What are the steps you need to take to get there? Where do you even find the beginning of that pathway which will allow you to begin the journey by taking those first tentative steps to work towards your goal and purpose that you want to achieve in life? Are you thinking this through as you are reading this and wondering where it could or should begin for you? Or do you already know where to begin?

Congratulations if you do! So, what's still holding you back from getting started then? In my experience, it usually comes down to your limiting self-beliefs in your own ability to achieve the goal. Is a fear of failure holding you back? The most common of these limiting beliefs are that you don't have enough time and/or don't have enough money. Sound familiar? Remember, if you want it badly enough, you will find the time and the money to make it happen. As the saying goes, *where there is a will, there is a way.* It's up to you to make it happen!

Unfortunately, most people don't know where to begin and the thoughts go round and round inside their heads without any action. It is often at this point, that most people stop thinking about it, they decide it is all too hard, and they give up. They don't know where or how to begin or who they might even talk to about pointing them in the right direction. They resign themselves to what they are currently doing and essentially, never start that journey to find the pathway to achieve their purpose in life.

It doesn't mean the desire to achieve the goal ever leaves them. It just means they never get started and eventually, one day when they are much older, they look back on their life and regret that they didn't go after their dream when they could have, but by that time it is often too late, and the dream remains just that – an unfulfilled dream. I believe it is better to have tried and failed than never to have tried at all. Then, at least, you can say, 'I gave it a go.'

It might surprise you to see that you actually succeed, just like the hundreds or thousands of people who have already taken that leap of faith, only to find that they really are capable of achieving their goals. Look at people like Mark Zuckerberg, Steve Jobs, Dolly Parton, just to name a few. You only need to search the internet to find hundreds of people who are self-made millionaires or billionaires. At some point, they all had to make a decision to give their dream a go. Some have come from abject poverty and have invested everything they had or owned to see their dream become reality.

For others who can't seem to bring themselves to take that first step to achieve their dreams they may already be considered by others to be successful in their life or career, but for them, it is that one elusive goal or dream they have for themselves, sitting deep in the back of their mind, which never really goes away, and which they never stop thinking about over the years. Yet, they never go after it, for the reasons I have mentioned above, or because they believe they are too busy to create the space. They need to begin the journey or seek out someone who can help them get started. They need an experienced life and mindset coach.

What is life coaching anyway?

Wikipedia defines Life Coaching as:

> '... the process of helping people identify and achieve personal goals through developing skills and attitudes that lead to self-empowerment. Life coaching generally deals with issues such as procrastination, fear of failure, relationship issues, lack of confidence, work–life balance and career changes, and often occurs outside the workplace setting' (Wikipedia, 2022).

A coach, in any field, is essentially someone who has the knowledge, ability, skills, and usually some formal qualifications in that field, to work with individuals to enable them to get started on their pathway towards achieving their goal with the coach's mentorship and encouragement. Together, they map out the steps needed to be taken to traverse the individualised and unique goal achievement journey or blueprint plan for the person being coached.

They work together to develop realistic and achievable steps to attain the desired purpose or goal. The coach then provides information and guidance while drawing on their own expertise, experience, and knowledge to assist their client while they continue to progress towards goal attainment. Coaches also hold their clients accountable through regular scheduled meetings to focus on progress made and achievements gained related to the plan, to that point in time. Essentially, this ensures maintaining accountability check points throughout the process, to ensure goals are eventually fully achieved. Analogous to the tough love of a parent for their child, this is like the kick up the bum that we all need some time.

Procrastination is always the enemy when working towards achieving goals. It is so important to have someone who will hold you accountable for the plans you have set for yourself. There are few people who will genuinely hold themselves accountable to meet their own planned goals within the expected timeframes, although these rare beasts, who have great intestinal fortitude, do exist. They are certainly the minority amongst us mere mortals.

Circling back to where I began this chapter, you have your purpose set plainly and clearly. You know what you want or need to do, but you don't know where to begin. This is where you research. You search the web for coaches in your area, or talk with other people, asking if they have a coach, or do they know a coach they would recommend to you. You will be amazed how many people already have a life coach or a mentor and it shouldn't take too long for you to be put in touch with a life and mindset coach. It is not something many people talk about openly as they feel it may be perceived as a limitation that anyone should need a coach. However, to the contrary, it shows a great honesty with yourself to be aware of your own strengths and limitations so you can seek the right coach to assist, support, nurture, and train you to develop in those areas for the purpose of achieving your ultimate life goal or goals.

Ideally, depending upon the goal you have set for yourself, it is best to find a life coach who has some experience or background in the area you need to be coached in. It is a personal preference for you to decide upon, whether it makes any difference to you if your coach needs to be of a particular gender, age, ethnicity, ability, religion, etc. These may be important, or not, depending upon what it is that you are seeking to achieve. Finding the right coach for you is key to ensuring you reach your desired goal. In these times of all things being much more accessible online, national and state borders do not limit us in who we can connect with and be coached by. Literally, the world is our oyster in terms of finding the right coach for each of us. There are thousands of coaches worldwide and one of them is the right coach for you. Of course, there will be fees involved for any coaching services, so you also need to do your research to weigh up costs and benefits of hiring any coach. Coaching fees will vary from coach to coach, depending on the intensity and length of the coaching agreement. Some may offer short term three month coaching packages, or six-month coaching packages or one year coaching packages. The costs may vary from a few hundred dollars to a few thousand dollars, depending upon the length of the agreement and the frequency of coaching services agreed upon. All of this can be personalised to meet individual needs, and these details are usually discussed with any potential coach at an initial no-cost meeting before any coaching agreement is reached. Coaching agreements are signed and can be binding for the period of time agreed upon. It is always important, as with any contract, to read it carefully before signing and seek legal advice if necessary. There is usually a cooling off period incorporated within the contract should a client change their mind for any reason. Whatever the ultimate coaching package agreed upon is, it is so important to consider the costs involved as investments in yourself and your future wellbeing and not as a type of financial burden.

People who have become successful in life have usually invested in their own self development at some time in their lives. No one gets to the top of their game in life without investing in themselves. Take note if your mindset is one of seeing money spent on yourself as a waste or as an investment in your future. Mindset is so important to the decisions we make in all aspects of our life. It can hold you back or propel you forwards depending on your beliefs. What is your mindset telling you now? *Are you thinking I could never spend thousands of dollars on myself to achieve my dreams?* Would you be happy to agree to spend thousands of dollars so your child or children can achieve their dreams? Or your partner achieves their dreams? If this is so, then why not you? Take note of your thinking as this is telling about your views towards money and whether you think you are worthy of spending money on yourself as freely as you might agree to for other loved ones in your life.

There are so many great books to help us understand our own mindset. One that I particularly like is written by world renowned Stanford University psychologist Carol S. Dweck, and it is titled *Mindset, The New Psychology of Success*. I recommend this book to anyone interested in delving into this topic further. If you are open to learn, it could change your life for the better.

When seeking a life coach for yourself, as it is with anyone you meet, there are some who you will immediately feel a connection with, or an affinity to after just a short period of time spent with them. This is an indication of alignment of values and worldviews between you and the other person. Take note of these connections as they are critical to success.

You may meet a coach who is highly credentialed and has extensive experience in the area you are seeking to aspire to, but if there is a mismatch of personalities and values and a lack of synergy or synchronicity between you both, it is not likely to be a good working partnership.

The message here is to find the right life coach for you and that may take a little searching but don't be afraid to interview your coach. Arrange to meet with them online, or face to face, and find out more about them and their background. Take note of how you feel about them when you are relating to them:

- Do you feel you can trust them?
- Are they someone who you immediately find to be relatable and likeable?
- Do they have credentials to back what they are saying with facts, figures, qualifications?
- Do they have runs on the board with other clients that can provide testimonials for the work they have done with them?

Big Hairy Audacious Goal

Talk to them about your area of interest and your specific goal and find out what experience and expertise they have in that field relevant to your goal. Then you can assess if they are the right person for you and whether you think you could work with them for weeks, months, or years, depending upon what your goal is and how long it may take to achieve.

When you find the right coach and you begin working with them, they will help you develop your coaching plan, as discussed in the previous chapter of this book. The plan will set out how you will work together to achieve your goal, over what timeframe, delineate the strategies for each step, and any resources you will need to successfully achieve your goal. Your coach will work with you to identify any other skills, knowledge, abilities, or technologies you will need to gain, learn, develop, or purchase for yourself to continuously improve and develop in your chosen area of endeavour.

To make this explanation more tangible and realistic, I will provide an example of what I am talking about from my experience of moving from having a long-standing career in the public service and the not-for-profit sector, into setting up and establishing my own consultancy, coaching, counselling business. I knew I had the knowledge, skills, and qualifications from the years of personal development, training, study, and career experience I had, however, I wasn't sure where to begin. So, I asked around and eventually found the right life coach for me.

It was the coaching methods and knowledge that I was most confident with. I knew I had years and years of training, life and career experience and knowledge to draw upon to successfully coach others. In fact, I had already been doing this for years as a friend or colleague, but not as a business for myself. So, these were not the areas of development which I needed. It was marketing, setting up technological and accounting systems and databases, advertising and running my own business that were the greatest challenges for me. I needed to learn how to use new software platforms to create and schedule social media posts, learn how to use promotional tools, and present my business and myself to the public to build my brand and generate an awareness about the coaching services I offer. I needed to get my name and my business known of and talked about and begin to develop business credibility, and relationships with potential clients. I needed to build trust with my audience and connect with my ideal clients.

I had a rapid learning trajectory but found all the people I needed to learn from. What I learnt was I needed to start freely sharing useful, helpful, life skills, knowledge, and information so those watching could see I knew what I was talking about. Thereby, helping them to get to know me better, and hopefully connecting with me or deciding they liked me or trusted me enough to want to find out more about me.

As I am a trained social worker, marketing was the last thing I ever had to think about throughout my career when I worked for government or the not-for-profit services. It was therefore, a very important area for my own business development, which I learned to embrace. It has been a steep learning curve since starting my business, and it still is. I have engaged marketing specialists to help me with this aspect of business, and it has been very worthwhile to do so.

Finding the right people to take on some of the business or administrative tasks and outsourcing these is so important. It has helped me to quickly get through a piece of work which would have otherwise taken me hours to complete. As a sole trader and business owner, I know that the time it takes to learn everything in a business is time away from the business. These may be sections of work that are not my strength areas and which I am not interested in taking the time to teach myself as it would take me too long. It is more cost effective to pay someone to do a piece of work in an area which they are very skilled and experienced in doing and can do in a fraction of the time and cost in which you could do it yourself. This is a very important lesson for any businessperson to learn.

When you find the right life coach for you, no matter what your goal is, you may find after a time of working together that you are taking the steps you need to begin achieving your goals and you begin to visualise how very achievable it is to reach the end prize, you will notice how focused you are. When this happens, you will also realise that you are living your passion and achieving your purpose and, in this moment, everything seems to become timeless. You are driven and focused and engrossed in what you are doing. You have found your purpose and flow. You could say you are in the groove, working in synergy with your coach. When this happens, you know you have the right coach for you.

In The Groove

So, what's holding you back now? The only thing stopping you is yourself, so get out of your own way, get out there, and get started!

'Not everybody can identify a purpose in life. But when you do, and when you pursue it, you will be living the kind of life you feel you were meant to live. And what's more, you will be happy.'
— **Steve Goodier**

Chapter 7

Wave Riding And Boundaries

Just as with everything in life, there are highs and lows. The ebb and flow of the waves of life create a rhythm which our psyche and our emotions react to throughout our lives. My philosophy in life is to enjoy the highs because you have reached the top of a particular phase or you have achieved a particular goal in your life and it is time to stop, appreciate, celebrate, and relish in the moment. While the lows are harder to ride through, the silver lining is in the knowing that there will be another high wave coming along before too long. Such is the way of life.

When we are living our life on purpose and we have been working with our coach for months or even years, we inevitably get to know them quite well and they also get to know us very well too. Just as with any relationship, the more honest and authentic you are with each other, the more the strengths and limitations of each other become apparent over time. Therefore, it is important for both the coach and the client to be mindful of consciously undertaking an evaluation of each other and the coaching relationship from time to time.

What I mean by this is, it is a good exercise to ask yourself, as the client, is my life coach still meeting my needs and what more do I need to learn to achieve my goal and what more can I learn from this coach? It's good to come up with a few points to write down which you can use as a guide to have a conversation with your coach about these things as there may be much more the coach can work with you to develop but it may not have been appropriate or the right timing in your self-development journey to learn new skills. The fact that you may now realise that there is more you need to learn is a good sign, as it indicates a higher level of self-awareness and self-development is growing within you.

Similarly, the coach may also ask themselves if there is more they need to work on developing with you to assist you in achieving your goal. They may also assess themselves in relation to what more you may need to learn, either from them or from someone else, and what more they know they have to offer you.

Keeping all of this in mind, it is important to realise it is possible to outgrow your coach when you have learnt as much from them as they can share with you, depending on what goal or goals you are working towards. I have known coaches who have worked with clients for several years and it is the coach who has suggested it is time for their client to find another life coach who can take them on the next phase of their goal attainment and personal development journey.

As we grow and evolve as humans, and we develop higher levels of knowledge and abilities with each goal we reach, it is important to start thinking about what the next goal is, big or small, that you want to achieve. For example, just as a young athlete may want to win a race at the school sports day, then aspire to win at a local, regional, and state championships, the higher-level goal may be to move on to win a race at the Commonwealth Games or at the Olympics and then it may change again, to become a coach of up-and-coming younger athletes. The habit to get into which will see you have a happy, purposeful, and fulfilling life is that you never stop setting

Wave Riding And Boundaries

and then achieving goals for yourself. These could be life, family, home, career, health, financial, educational, relationship, business, or any number of numerous other goal possibilities. They could be monumental, like starting a new business or enrolling in a PhD or tiny goals, such starting an exercise program. The choices are yours to make, but the key here is to be consciously making goals and then achieving them, over and over.

Our goals are not static and as we continue to work, improve, and strive to achieve each higher-level goal, the coach we are working with also needs to be at the next level of knowledge to continuously stretch and challenge us. This will help us strive higher and higher to achieve to our fullest potential. Of course, it goes without saying, the coach can only do so much, as the heavy lifting and hard work to achieve the goal sits squarely with you, the client.

The relationship between ourselves and our coach inevitably will grow in depth and connectedness over time, as more and more information is shared between the two of you as you work together. This is necessary and important for the relationship to be a fruitful and rewarding one to achieve the expected goal attainment outcomes.

As with any two people in a working relationship it is important to be conscious of the necessity of having and maintaining boundaries. It is important to know that each partner in the coaching relationship has a life outside of that relationship with other work, life, and family commitments. It is very important to discuss, at the commencement of the working agreement, what the boundaries are in terms of contacting each other outside of scheduled coaching appointments. This should ideally all be set out clearly in a formal coaching agreement or contract, which each party agrees to and signs off on at the commencement of the coaching partnership.

For example, life coaches usually have many clients they are working with, either one-on-one or within group settings. They are usually also developing coaching program content for either online courses they offer or for planned group workshops or other events. Clients also have very busy lives as they usually have family, work, sporting, educational, and other social commitments while also working towards achieving their life goals plan. Therefore, it is necessary to respect each other's space and time away from scheduled coaching appointments.

Usually, life coaches and their clients will have an agreement or contract in place which outlines agreed to processes to contact each other outside of scheduled appointment times. This is very important, otherwise each person could be encroaching on whatever the other is doing at any given time. Imagine the time impacts of this for a coach who has many clients, if such an agreement was not in place. It is often agreed upon by both parties that contact can be made between scheduled appointments via email or SMS, rather than making a phone call, holding a face-to-face meeting or a zoom call, unless there is something urgent which comes up which requires a phone or face-to-face conversation but even then, it is important to have a clause in the agreement which covers these types of unanticipated situations.

Wave Riding And Boundaries

Maintaining agreed to boundaries indicates respect for the other party and their families and whatever else they may have happening in their lives at any given time. This is so important for the coaching relationship to flourish. You could imagine if one or the other person was making unplanned contact and calling all the time, how that could become disruptive, because of the constant interruptions of whatever else they may be doing.

The basis of any healthy relationship, whether that be a personal or work relationship, is to demonstrate mutual respect. By being considerate of each other's time outside of the coaching relationship, you convey the message that I care enough about you that I respect your time outside of our time together. This makes for a very positive and fruitful working relationship and allows for rejuvenation so each partner can approach their next time together with enthusiasm, motivation, and eagerness.

> *'When you respect someone, you make a conscious choice to not cross their boundaries. Regardless of the type of relationship that you have with one another.'*
> — **Robin S. Baker**

Chapter 8

Celebrating Your Wins

In life there are many important events which are celebrated through the processes of symbolic rituals. This includes things like christenings, finishing high school, getting married, milestone birthdays, even funerals where a life is celebrated. The importance of rituals is so important to our sense of self and our identities, such as moving from being a student to being a worker in the workforce or getting married from being a single person. If you think about the ritual (either formal or informal) which takes place, it instils a sense of moving and evolution in life, a time of something ending and something else beginning. These times allow us to reflect on where we have come from and what we have achieved e.g., graduating from university, becoming someone's wife or husband. It is powerful and can change the psychology of our identity.

These ritualistic points serve an important purpose in life as they create the opportunity to tangibly bring the realisation that we are changing from one state and moving into another. It provides us with a point in time in our lives, usually with photos to mark the event which we relate back on over subsequent years.

In previous chapters, I have talked about the importance of celebrating your goal achievements. This can be when you hit an important milestone along the goal attainment journey, or when you finally reach that ultimate goal, you have been working towards for so long, and then – you're there, you've done it! For me, it was when I graduated from university with my PhD which took years to complete and to me felt like my Mt. Everest to climb, but in the end, I got there, and I was so excited. After the formal ritual of attending a graduation ceremony, I celebrated this goal achievement with my friends and family by going out to dinner and having some celebratory drinks. It was such a happy event for me.

Many people who are high achievers in life don't take the time to stop and celebrate their achievements because they are already focused on the next big goal they have their eye on to achieve. They don't allow themselves the time to take a breath and soak in the significance and euphoria of the moment, but doing so is so important, not just for self-adulation or experiencing an intense feeling of satisfaction and achievement but for so much more than that as well.

I have had several friends who have been studying at postgraduate level and when talking with them they have stated they didn't think they would go to their graduation ceremony. I urged them to reconsider, as it is an opportunity that doesn't come along every day, and it is a day they will never forget. Two of my friends graduated with their doctorates at different times. Both told me they thought they wouldn't go to the trouble of attending the graduation ceremony, but I talked to them about the importance, not only for themselves, but for their families and others, to enjoy the celebration with them. Interestingly, they both went on to attend their respective graduation ceremonies and both thanked me for encouraging them to do so as they said it was a wonderful achievement which their families could participate in and for their children to see their hard work paying off and the celebration of their efforts over many years.

Celebrating Your Wins

There is also evidence that celebrating our achievements is good for our brain and our overall general wellbeing (Gutheridge, 2019). In that moment of realisation that we have achieved what we set out to, we can experience feelings of excitement, exuberance, exhilaration, happiness, joy, relief, and so many more emotions. This is because at these times the brain releases dopamine, which is a feel-good neurotransmitting chemical that flows throughout our bodies creating high excitement and euphoria. When this happens, your brain takes note of what has just caused this wonderful feeling of elation, as it will seek to replicate it again in the future.

Dopamine helps us to feel pleasure, and it helps us to focus, learn with clarity, strive to improve, and feel motivated towards achieving repeatedly, thereby replicating the pleasurable experience. It has so many physical and psychological benefits to our overall health and our sense of physical and mental wellbeing. However, a word of caution is needed here because too much dopamine is not good for us either. It can lead to addictions of all types to re-experience the euphoric feelings when they're not occurring naturally or frequently enough, it can affect weight gain, or cause aggression. There are several other negative side effects too (Cohen, 2022). The message here is that it is important and exciting to celebrate wins. But, as with most things in life, all things need to be done in moderation, so they don't end up becoming self-destructive.

Getting the balance right is critical to our overall success. When working to achieve your goal it is also necessary to stop sometimes and ensure you are making time for

Big Hairy Audacious Goal

the other important people and activities in your life which will help to maintain good personal relationships and monitoring our exercise levels and diet to keep fit, well and healthy. Again, getting the balance right between all these important elements is key to enabling you to continue to strive towards achieving your ultimate goal, whatever that may be.

When we do stop to celebrate our successes, it is good to take stock of, reflect on, and evaluate what we have done so far that has worked well during the process, what didn't work so well, and what we would do differently when we start to work towards our next big goal. This is how we learn from our experiences as we again move forward towards the next large or small goal, we set for ourselves. It can motivate us and provide a sense of achievement of how far we have come to reach that point. It is likely to illicit feelings of appreciation and recognition of your own continuous improvement and self-development, and reinforce your sense of self belief, which is a critical factor in achieving personal or professional goals in life.

Self-belief builds confidence and self-esteem. It helps us to move past having a fear of failure, or a fear of success, or experiencing imposter syndrome because we have proved to ourselves and to others that we not only can achieve big goals we set for ourselves but that we have done so, or are doing so. This then, affects our mindset positively because we stop doubting whether we can achieve goals in our life, and we move towards the realisation that we can, and in fact we are, achieving them with the right coaching support, and developing the necessary knowledge, skills, and abilities.

Celebrating Your Wins

Each time we set ourselves a new goal, it is inevitable that there are new skills we will also need to attain, broadening our repertoire of abilities, and in doing so, a new sense of interest, challenge, and ultimately mastery, is created. Thereby providing us with a deep sense of accomplishment and fulfilment. All good for our own sense of purpose and self.

Another advantage of celebrating your wins is that you are always being watched and noticed by others around you. Without it necessarily being your intention, you are serving as a role model for others in your life and community. This would especially include your own children or other young people in your extended family or community who are watching what you are doing and what you are achieving.

When others see someone succeeding and achieving a particular goal, it can inspire others to do the same. You see it repeatedly in the sporting world, in particular after the Olympics or some other high profile sporting event, children say they want to be like a standout sporting hero, but it also applies within all other fields of endeavour.

Relationships can also be strengthened when others closest to you feel a sense of pride in what you have achieved. They feel good and are proud to acknowledge your hard work, dedication, and achievements to others, often to our embarrassment. The influence you can have without even knowing it can be monumental in the longer term. It is like the ripple effect of a pebble being thrown into a pond. The points where the ripples touch are wide and often way beyond what anyone could have anticipated.

Big Hairy Audacious Goal

Without you even consciously thinking about it, you are influencing others who are watching. You are setting an example for all those around you which proves anything is possible, if you have self-belief, maintain focus, never give up, and work consistently and diligently towards achieving a particular goal, you will achieve it. The celebration of such a huge achievement is a tangible and visible event. The mere celebration says to others, look what I have achieved, and the subliminal message is that you can achieve your goals too. It is possible for you to do this too. So, it can inspire others and this osmosis effect occurs and serves to lift the community overall. When we see others achieve something that we greatly admire, like being successful in any field, then that says anyone can do this and others aspire to do the same. It improves the overall quality of life for all in the community.

Have you ever thought of your achievements and the potential impact they can have within the bigger picture of life as I have just outlined? Few people do, but it is important to stop and realise what effect can be gained from your goal setting, working hard to achieve it, then celebrating your wins or successes can have, not only for yourself, but for your family, and the broader community.

'Success is best when it is shared'
— **Howard Schultz**

Chapter 9

Changing Lanes

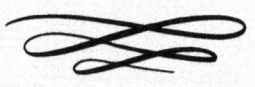

Previous chapters of this book have focused on the steps and processes necessary to identify your goals and how to find a coach who is the right fit for you. So, imagine you have followed these steps and identified your goal, and you found the right life coach for you, and you have been working with them for some time and you might even have achieved the goal you set out to. Then you have taken the time out to celebrate your successes which, as I have written about in previous chapters is such an important aspect of the whole goal achievement process, so don't skip the celebration, you've worked hard to achieve your goals, so celebrate the moment with your nearest and dearest.

Sometimes it is apparent and logical that completing a certain goal we have set for ourselves inevitably leads naturally onto the next goal you can clearly see for yourself. You might know exactly what it is that you want to do next.

For example, when I first began studying, I enrolled in an associate diploma which I diligently worked on, part time, by distance education for four years. Now when I began this course, my goal was just to complete the course, but as I got nearer to the finish line, I was already thinking about what I wanted to do next. I knew I wanted to enrol in a Social Work bachelor's degree. To do this, my husband and I and our three young children needed to relocate to Townsville so I could attend university full time. This is what we did and to this day, we have no regrets that we took this big step.

So, when you are working on your big goal for yourself the next logical step may become very apparent, and this is great when this happens, and it is so clear to you. However, for others the next step or goal may not be as clear, and it may take some time to think about what it is you want to do next, or it may be something which would never have occurred to you, but it just seems to present itself to you. Just as my earlier experience of attending a book writing workshop, to investigate what is involved in writing and publishing my own book and the next thing I know is the presenter starts talking about the book being a springboard for our own businesses. For me, this was completely left field, as setting up a business was never in my line of sight as a goal for myself. However, I kept an open mind and continued the book writing journey, which eventually led me to seriously consider developing my own business as an author, speaker, coach, and counsellor. None of these possibilities were ever what I dreamt I would be doing. Even writing a book in the first place was something others had encouraged me to do initially yet it was completed and now you are reading my second book, which also, was never on the horizon for me but again, was suggested to me based on my successful coaching business. This is where the importance of keeping an open mind about possibilities and options that present themselves to us is critical to our ongoing successes.

In chapter one of this book, I talked about how I see my business as being my fourth career, one I never anticipated having, but here I am doing what I love and loving what I do. It is achievable for anyone who seeks to live their dreams, as outlined in the previous chapters of this book.

Changing Lanes

In my fourth career, I feel that I have completely changed lanes in life and career. I have moved into the world of commerce, sales, and marketing, which are such critical aspects of running a business that I had to master or bring on consultants to learn from or to do the work for me.

This chapter is about the possibilities of actually changing lanes in life. By this I mean you again take a leap of faith to move into a completely different field of work or area of interest and set yourself a goal in this new space. You could be someone who has always worked in a certain field, let's say, for example, in an office and you take a huge step by moving into a construction role by starting an adult apprenticeship. Or you could be a construction worker who decides to take up pottery or floristry. Something very removed and different from what you have always done is the point of these examples.

To do this, you may need to face your inner fears by taking the step to do some work on yourself to develop your self-confidence, and build your self-esteem, or learn to believe in yourself and your abilities to succeed. You may also need to examine your mindset and ensure you are operating from a mindset which is not fixed, but to one which is open to learn and take a chance to try out new possibilities.

Here are some famous people who completely changed their careers to become extremely successful in their newly chosen career or field of endeavour:

Big Hairy Audacious Goal

- Jeff Bezos had a lucrative career in computer science on Wall Street and took on top roles at various financial firms before transitioning to the world of e-commerce and launching Amazon at 31.

- Vera Wang was a figure skater and journalist before entering the fashion industry at age 40. Today she's one of the world's premier women's designers.

- Billionaire Spanx founder Sara Blakely sold office supplies door-to-door for seven years in her 20s before her line of slimming footless pantyhose launched to success in 2000. She quit her sales job at 30 to run her company full-time.

- Arnold Schwarzenegger has made two major career changes, first when he transitioned from world champion bodybuilder in his 20s to award-winning actor in his 30s, then when he became the Governor of California in 2003 at 56.

- Ray Kroc spent his career as a milkshake-device salesman before buying McDonalds at age 52 in 1954. He grew it into the world's biggest fast-food franchise.

The key message here is that changing lanes can have some amazing results, but if you are too afraid to give something a go, you will never know. It often takes some form of severe adversity for people to feel desperate enough to plunge themselves into trying out something completely different in life. Yet it is usually the desperation of the situation and the determination to not fail or give up that sees these people succeed. Hard work, self-belief, commitment, consistency to keep showing up, and dedication to the ultimate goal is what will lead to the ultimate success. All these things are critical to succeed, along with doing your research into what has worked before for others in the same or other fields of endeavour, rather than reinvent the wheel and make the same mistakes again. Might as well take the path of least resistance rather than making the journey harder than it needs to be.

The main point here, though, is to recognise your fears, face them head on, then jump in and go after your goal with one hundred percent commitment and be prepared to give your goal the time it needs to manifest. Too often we give up too soon. Expect setbacks, as they are part of the journey, learn from them each time and go again. Follow your goal achievement plan, work with your coach, and never give up. All the people listed above would never have reached their goals if they had given up and look at what they have achieved.

> *'If you never try, you'll never know what you are capable of.'*
> **John Barrow**

Chapter 10

Never Give Up

You will recall at the beginning of this book I talked about self-beliefs and mindset, both of which are so critical to achieving in life. As I mentioned in earlier chapters if you believe you can do something and you have a drive, determination, passion, and the motivation to achieve your goal, then the chances are you are likely to do so because you will find a way, when others in similar positions may give up.

What makes the difference between those who have a dream, or a goal and they strive to achieve it but before too long they decide it's all too hard and they give up and those people who have the same struggles and obstacles in their way but time and time again they always find a way around them? They never accept they can't achieve their goal and they don't ever give up. They have the guts, grit, and determination to find a way to make their dream become a reality. They have and maintain high levels of tenacity and resilience in the face of any roadblocks thrown at them, but somehow, they keep going, they never give up. They find the right person to assist them, or they research areas where the blockages are occurring to find new ways of doing things so they can keep moving forward. Step by step, obstacle by obstacle, they find their way to the end of the journey to ultimately achieve their goal.

Think about all those people who achieve amazing feats in their respective areas of passion, no matter what these may be. It could be to climb the highest mountain, start a business, grow a business to the next level, become a healthier version of themselves, complete their uni course or degree, build or rebuild important relationships

Big Hairy Audacious Goal

in their lives, grow their wealth, set up a charity, or any other goal which you could imagine.

There will always be people who will tell you you're crazy or question why you would want to achieve a particular goal (because it's not something they would ever want to do). These people will always exist to tell you all the reasons why you should not strive to achieve your goal and if we doubt ourselves even minimally, these types of comments can plant the seeds of self-doubt. Then we may start questioning ourselves about whether we should, in fact, be pursuing our dream or goal. However, if there is one very clear message, I hope you will take away with you from reading this book, it is to believe in yourself and do not listen to all the people in life who will quickly tell you all the reasons why you should not pursue your particular goal. It may even be those nearest and dearest to you, that will make these types of comments, usually from a place of good intent, however, because they are those closest to us, they can and often do, influence what we believe ourselves to be capable of. I am sure they believe they have your self-interests at heart, but they are not you. They do not know what your deepest held dreams and goals are or feel the desire to achieve these goals as deeply as you do.

I once wanted to apply for a manager's job. It was a very high-pressure position within the field of child protection within the government. I worked in this field for sixteen years, so I knew exactly how hard, challenging, complex and difficult this area of work really is. There was a high turnover of staff because of the pressures of working within this environment. It is a particularly thankless job because it mostly happens behind closed doors because of the sensitive nature of the work and it is only ever when something goes horribly wrong that the media highlight the work of child protection workers. It carries a very negative stigma to be working in this field, as no matter what decisions or actions are made, they will always be the wrong ones from someone's perspective.

I had so many people say to me, why would you want to do that job, what are you thinking, are you crazy? I am sure you are also probably thinking these same thoughts as you read this now. The reason I wanted to apply for that job was that I believed I could make a difference for the better in the lives of children who had experienced severe abuse or neglect, whether or not I did is open to speculation. There have been some children who, as adults, have told me I did have a positive influence on their lives, but who knows about the hundreds of others in the system? I will never know, I guess. Another reason I wanted that job was that it was another upward step on the rung of my career ladder, which I was ambitious to attain.

Of all the people I spoke to when I was considering applying for that position, there was only one person who encouraged me to go for it if it was truly what I wanted to do. Her advice to me was so heartening, particularly when everyone else was discouraging me. However, as I am not someone who likes to have regrets or be left to wonder about what would have happened if I hadn't applied, I did apply for the position and was fortunate enough to have got it. This was a role I went on to fulfil for the next five years. I learned so much from that job,

Big Hairy Audacious Goal

which has always stayed with me, and I have taken and used the experience gained there in so many other stages of my career and life. I am so grateful to have had the opportunity to do that work and so grateful to that one person who encouraged me to go after it.

Sometimes you will also have that one person who encourages you to go after your goals in life, but then there are other times when there will be no one cheering you on. In these situations, you need to listen to your inner self talk. My recommendation is to think on it, sleep on it, and spend time pondering and considering what it is that you want to do. You may need to undertake some research on the topic, or you may need to speak to someone who has expertise or experience in that particular area. In short, you need to do your homework. But if you have done all of that and you still have a deep desire to pursue your goal, then listen to yourself and go after your dream.

As mentioned in previous chapters, it is very advisable to seek out a mentor or coach to help you achieve your goals but after you have been working with a coach or mentor for some time, maybe even years, you may realise that your self-beliefs have become much more positive, and you now feel confident that you know how to achieve your goal by yourself. You may find that it is time to branch out on your own to continue working towards achieving your goal. In these instances, you will need to learn to be your own best coach. Listen to your own self-talk. Those conversations you have with yourself in your head about what you are doing or what you are going to do, about whether you talk yourself out of doing things or talk yourself into doing things? Ask yourself:

Never Give Up

Are the messages I give to myself positive and encouraging messages, just like those I would give to my best friend who needed to hear them, or are they more negative conversations about all the reasons I can't or shouldn't even be thinking about what I would really like to be doing?

Are you talking yourself out of achieving your dreams and goals in life or finding all the reasons you should do them?

Take note of these conversations you have with yourself and note whether you feel confident to get on with focusing on your goals by yourself or whether you still feel too scared to step out of your comfort zone? If this is what you notice about yourself, this is an indication that you need to be strengthening your self-belief, changing your mindset to a more positive position, building self-confidence and self-esteem. If this is the case, then maybe you do still need to be working with a coach. However, if you feel strong and confident to pursue your goals by yourself, then you have learned to become your own best coach and you can probably focus and continue to work towards achieving the next goal you have set for yourself on your own. Remember, finding another coach is always possible if needed.

As you can see, setting and achieving goals is a lifelong process for anyone who seeks to achieve to their highest potential in life. As mentioned in earlier chapters, successful people are always working towards achieving the next goal they set for themselves. The cycle of success is to set a goal, plan how to achieve that goal, take action, evaluate progress, re-set goal, take action and repeat. I have developed the *5 A's to Life Achievement* cycle, which is illustrated below.

I use this model to work with the clients I coach in my business. I begin by working with them to assist them in assessing what is important in life for them and what goal or goals they want to achieve for themselves. Once their goal has been identified the next step is to undertake a planning process with the client during which the steps needed to be undertaken are planned and developed using the SMART goals approach as outlined in chapter five. This forms the blueprint for the pathway forward to achieve their goal. Once this work has been completed, the client then affirms the goal before the work begins to achieve it.

The steps of my model, the **5 A's to Life Achievement** are outlined below:

- **Assess** the goal they want to achieve.
- **Affirm** through the planning process that the goal and the plan to achieve it are what the client is committed to doing.
- **Action** then has to be taken to work towards achieving the goal.
- **Appraisal** is necessary at regular intervals to review progress made, to evaluate work undertaken to that point, to re-set any aspects of the plan that may need to be adjusted or changed in any way, then keep going.
- **Accomplish** the goal through consistency and diligence to ultimately achieve the goal.

Big Hairy Audacious Goal

Of course, when this stage has been reached it is time to celebrate the accomplishments and the hard work it has taken to get to that point. Then the cycle repeats as much as any person wishes to achieve for themselves. You will have developed the power within yourself, the positive self-beliefs, and the growth mindset to take on whatever goal you next set for yourself.

If you have read all of this book, you are obviously someone who seeks to have a fulfilling life, someone who has goals to be achieved, and a desire to make them become a reality. I have provided you with the strategies, tips, tools, guides and examples to help you get started on your own goal achievement journey.

In chapter two, you identified the most important goals for yourself to achieve, so my question or challenge to you is, what steps are you now going to take to achieve them?

If you don't take action now, then when will you take it? What excuses are you going to make for not taking action? Too old, too young, not enough money, not enough time, not the right time etc. etc. etc. If you don't ever take steps to achieve your goals, they will always remain your goals and dreams and nothing more – ever!

> **'Life's rewards go to those who let their actions rise above their excuses.'**
>
> Lee J. Colan

About The Author

Dr Anne Butcher is a life and mindset coach for women, an entrepreneur, and a businesswoman. She is a professional social worker and runs her own counselling practice. She has more than 30 years of experience working in the social welfare fields of Community Development, Youth Development, Youth Justice, Child Protection, Disability Services, Women's Services - including domestic violence and sexual assault counselling services, and women's health and wellbeing programs.

A social researcher, university lecturer, and the author of academic journal articles, book chapters and books. She is regularly asked to speak at conferences and significant community events such as International Women's Day, and to a range of other women's groups, service clubs, and community groups. Anne has worked as an executive director, manager and leader, in government and in not for profit organisations. She has also held positions on national, state and regional boards in Queensland and Australia.

Anne is passionate about seeing people, particularly girls and women, succeed in their lives and reach their fullest potential.

Anne has regularly featured on the ABC, Channel 7 and in The Courier Mail.

She is an engaging, motivational, and inspiring event speaker. Her speaking engagements demonstrate her warm, humorous, and personable speaking style. Her focus is to inspire and motivate others to achieve their life's dreams and goals through sharing her own depth of coaching knowledge and of her own life stories about work, study, and family.

Anne's speaking events are not to be missed and will leave her audience inspired to take action to achieve in their own life.

She can be contacted on:
E: anne@drannebutcher.com
W: drannebutcher.com

Reference List

Dopamine: What is it & What it Does? Accessed at: https://www.webmd.com/mental-health/what-is-dopamine

Doran, G., Miller, A., Cunningham, J. (1981) There's a S.M.A.R.T. way to write management's goals and objectives. Management Review (AMA Forum), November, 1981.

Dweck, C. S. (2008). *Mindset, The New Psychology of Success*. Ballantine Books, New York.

Guthridge, L. (2019) Recently Succeed at Something? Celebrating is Good For your Brain. Accessed at:

https://www.forbes.com/sites/forbescoachescouncil/2019/06/24/recently-succeed-at-something-celebrating-is-good-for-your-brain/?sh=5995b5073d91

What is Dopamine & Is It Bad in Excess? Accessed at: https://health.selfdecode.com/blog/dopamine-definition-excess/

Wikipedia - *Life Coaching*. Accessed at: https://en.wikipedia.org/wiki/Coaching#Life

Offers And Call To Action

Offer 1. To learn more about how to set your own life goals and take care of your own physical, psychological, emotional, and financial destiny. I have prepared three short helpful videos for you to access, at no cost on my website: www.drannebutcher.com

Offer 2. Engage Dr Anne Butcher as your next event speaker!

Anne speaks on the following topics:

1. Steps to take to move from where you are, to living your best life.

2. How to overcome self-limiting beliefs and build your confidence.

3. Overcoming barriers to succeed.

Offer 3. Register for my *Empowered Women Series* of online courses to achieve your big hairy audacious goal. Go to my website to register www.drannebutcher.com

Notes

Big Hairy Audacious Goal

Notes

Big Hairy Audacious Goal

Notes

www.ingramcontent.com/pod-product-compliance
Lightning Source LLC
Chambersburg PA
CBHW041145110526
44590CB00027B/4133